How to draw AMONG US

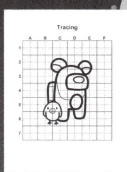

3 in 1

...SUS

Among US coloring book

Introduction

Disclaimer

No part of this publication may be reproduced in whole or in part, or stored in a retrieval system or transmitted in any form or by any means, electronic, mechanical,photocopying, recording or otherwise, without prior permission of the author.

Buy One Get One Free

Get a bonus at the end of book

Free Activity Book for Kids (PDF DOWNLOAD)

How to draw
AMONG US

IMPOSTOR

Coloring book for kids

This book belong to

_____

How to draw Among us

Step 01

Step by Step 1 To 4

Step 02

Step 03

Coloring Among Us

Step 04

How to draw Among us

Step 01

Step by Step 1 To 4

Step 02

Step 03

Coloring Among Us

Step 04

How to draw Among us

Step 01

Step by Step 1 To 4

Step 02

Step 03

Coloring Among Us

Step 04

How to draw Among us

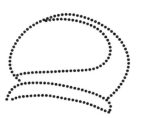

Step by Step 1 To 4

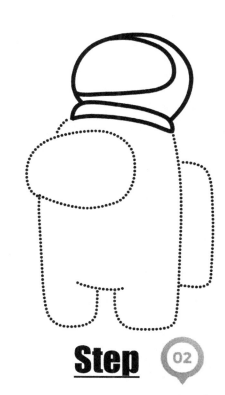

Step 01

Step 02

Step 03

Coloring Among Us

Step 04

How to draw Among us

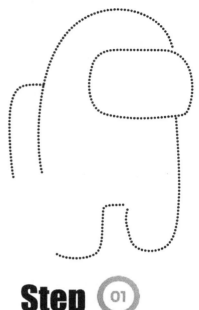

Step 01

Step 02

Step 03

Coloring Among Us

Step 04

How to draw Among us

Step by Step 1 To 4

Step 01

Step 02

Step 03

Coloring Among Us

Step 04

How to draw Among us

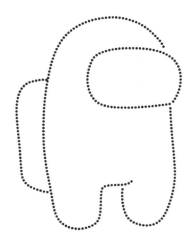

Step 01

Step by Step 1 To 4

Step 02

Step 03

Coloring Among Us

Step 04

How to draw Among us

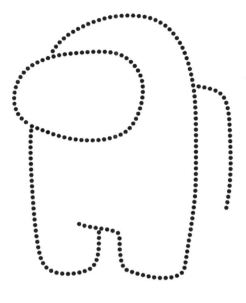

Step 01

Step by Step 1 To 4

Step 02

Step 03

Coloring Among Us

Step 04

How to draw Among us

Step 01

Step by Step 1 To 4

Step 02

Step 03

Coloring Among Us

Step 04

How to draw Among us

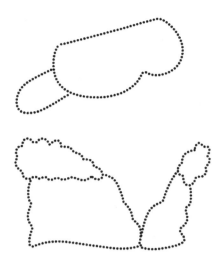

Step 01

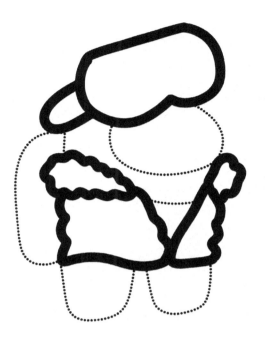

Step 02

Step 03

Coloring Among Us

Step 04

How to draw Among us

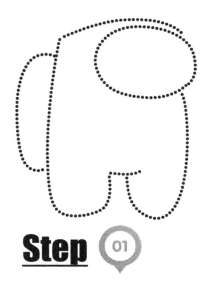

Step 01

Step 02

Step 03

Coloring Among Us

Step 04

How to draw Among us

Step by Step 1 To 4

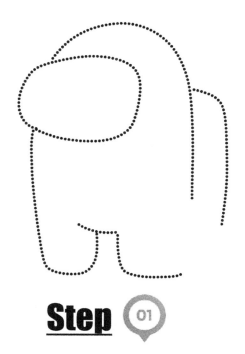

Step 01

Step 02

Step 03

Coloring Among Us

Step 04

How to draw Among us

Step by Step 1 To 4

Step 01

Step 02

Step 03

Coloring Among Us

Step 04

How to draw Among us

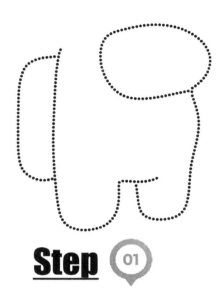

Step 01

Step 02

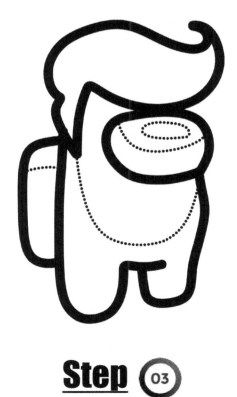

Step 03

Coloring Among Us

Step 04

How to draw Among us

Step by Step 1 To 4

Step 01

Step 02

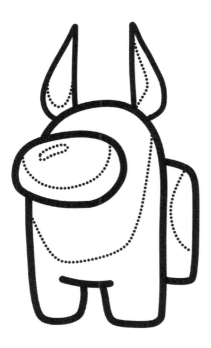

Step 03

Coloring Among Us

Step 04

How to draw Among us

Step 01

Step by Step 1 To 4

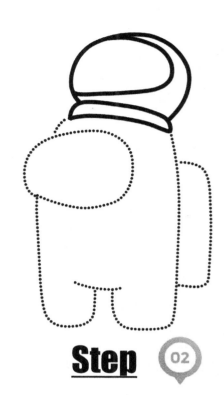

Step 02

Step 03

Coloring Among Us

Step 04

Beginner Level

Tracing

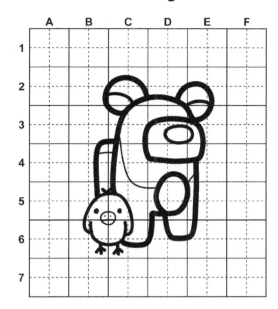

Step 1. Grid Example

Your tract!

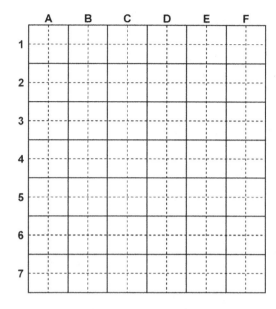

Step 2. Draw Follow Grid Line

Advance Level

Draw it!

Step 1 Image Example

Your own!

Step 2. Draw Follow Image

Beginner Level

Tracing

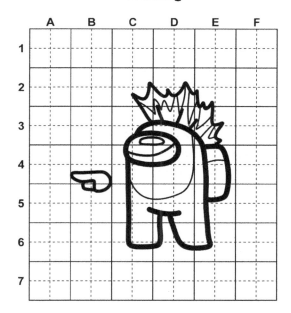

A B C D E F

1 2 3 4 5 6 7

Step 1.Grid Example

Your tract!

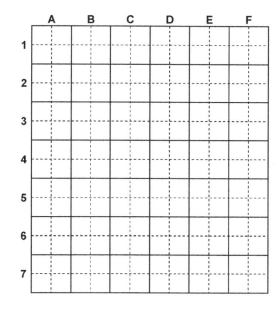

A B C D E F

1 2 3 4 5 6 7

Step 2. Draw Follow Grid Line

Advance Level

Draw it!

Step 1 Image Example

Your own!

Step 2. Draw Follow Image

Beginner Level

Tracing

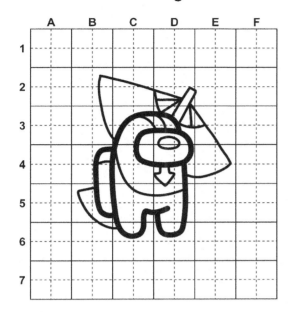

Step 1.Grid Example

Your tract!

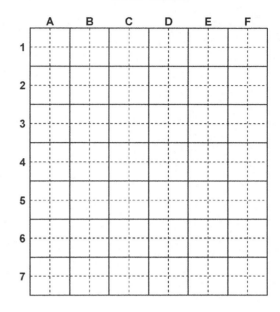

Step 2. Draw Follow Grid Line

Advance Level

Draw it!

Step 1 Image Example

Your own!

Step 2. Draw Follow Image

Beginner Level

Tracing

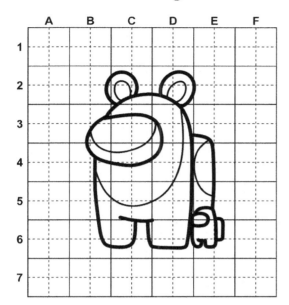

Step 1.Grid Example

Your tract!

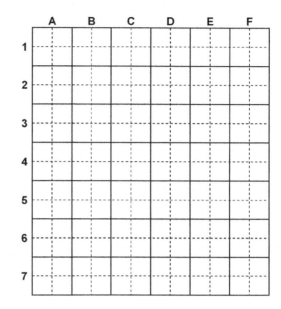

Step 2. Draw Follow Grid Line

Advance Level

Draw it!

Step 1 Image Example

Your own!

Step 2. Draw Follow Image

Beginner Level

Tracing

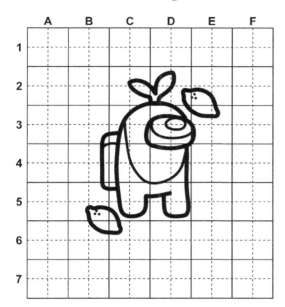

Step 1. Grid Example

Your tract!

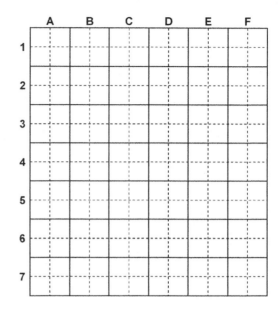

Step 2. Draw Follow Grid Line

Advance Level

Draw it!

Step 1 Image Example

Your own!

Step 2. Draw Follow Image

Beginner Level

Tracing

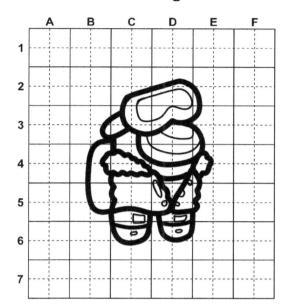

Step 1.Grid Example

Your tract!

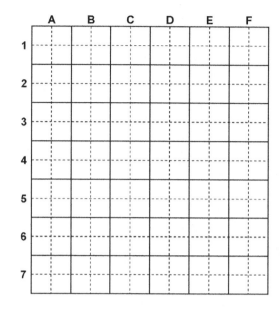

Step 2. Draw Follow Grid Line

Advance Level

Draw it!

Step 1 Image Example

Your own!

Step 2. Draw Follow Image

Beginner Level

Tracing

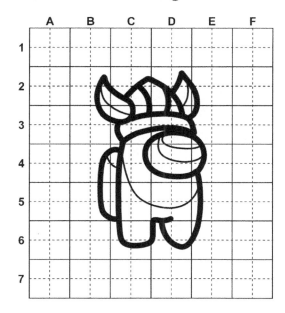

Step 1.Grid Example

Your tract!

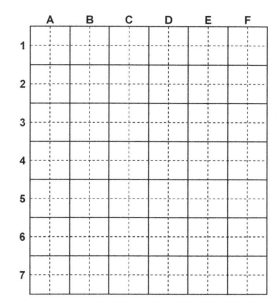

Step 2. Draw Follow Grid Line

Advance Level

Draw it!

Step 1 Image Example

Your own!

Step 2. Draw Follow Image

Beginner Level

Tracing

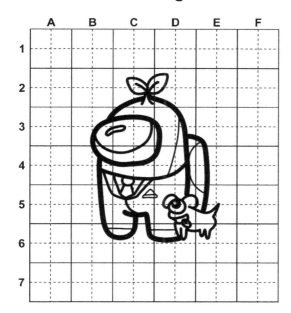

Step 1.Grid Example

Your tract!

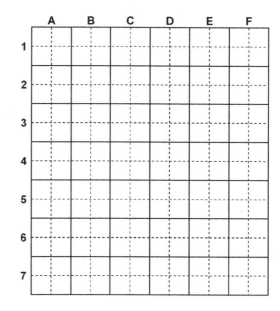

Step 2. Draw Follow Grid Line

Advance Level

Draw it!

Step 1 Image Example

Your own!

Step 2. Draw Follow Image

Beginner Level

Tracing

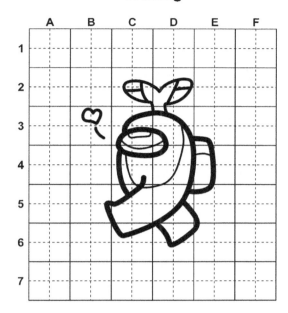

Step 1. Grid Example

Your tract!

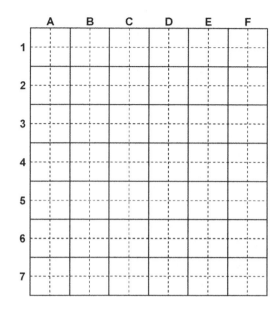

Step 2. Draw Follow Grid Line

Advance Level

Draw it!

Step 1 Image Example

Your own!

Step 2. Draw Follow Image

Beginner Level

Tracing

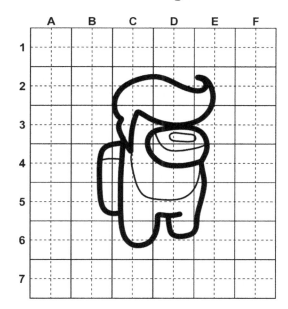

Step 1.Grid Example

Your tract!

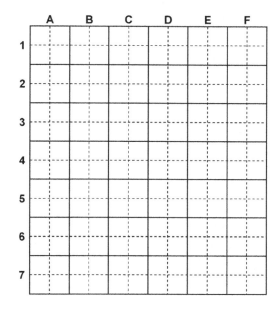

Step 2. Draw Follow Grid Line

Advance Level

Draw it!

Step 1 Image Example

Your own!

Step 2. Draw Follow Image

Beginner Level

Tracing

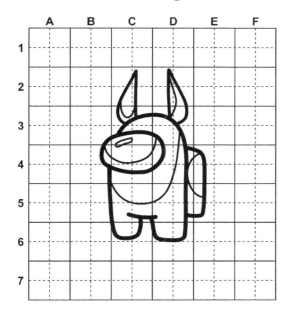

Step 1. Grid Example

Your tract!

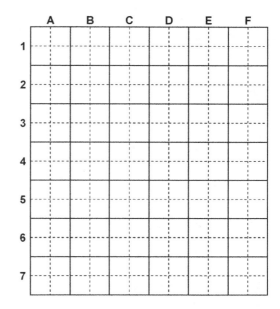

Step 2. Draw Follow Grid Line

Advance Level

Draw it!

Step 1 Image Example

Your own!

Step 2. Draw Follow Image

Beginner Level

Tracing

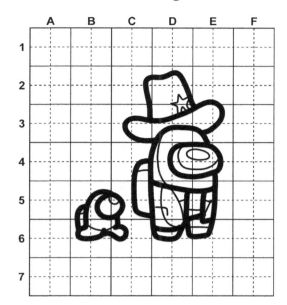

Step 1.Grid Example

Your tract!

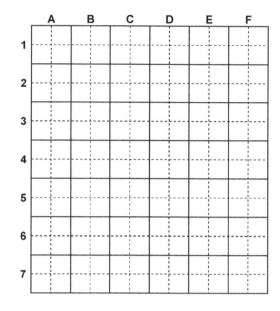

Step 2. Draw Follow Grid Line

Advance Level

Draw it!

Step 1 Image Example

Your own!

Step 2. Draw Follow Image

Beginner Level

Tracing

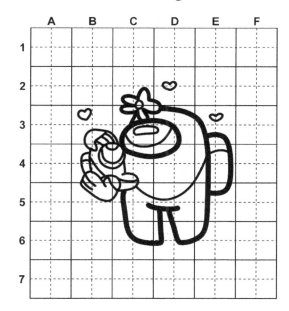

Step 1. Grid Example

Your tract!

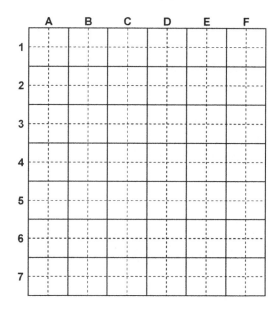

Step 2. Draw Follow Grid Line

Advance Level

Draw it!

Step 1 Image Example

Your own!

Step 2. Draw Follow Image

Beginner Level

Tracing

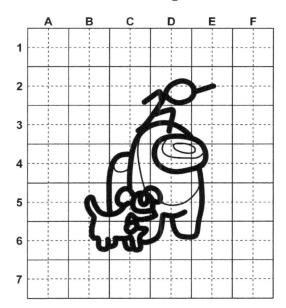

Step 1.Grid Example

Your tract!

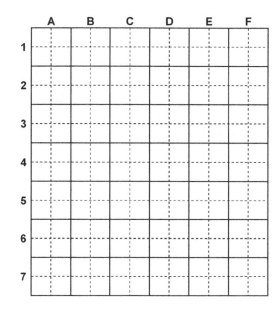

Step 2. Draw Follow Grid Line

Advance Level

Draw it!

Step 1 Image Example

Your own!

Step 2. Draw Follow Image

Beginner Level

Tracing

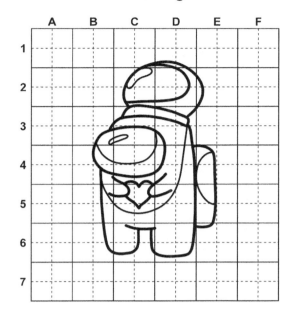

Step 1. Grid Example

Your tract!

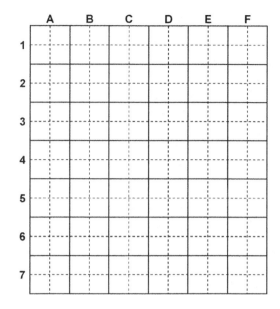

Step 2. Draw Follow Grid Line

Advance Level

Draw it!

Step 1 Image Example

Your own!

Step 2. Draw Follow Image

Beginner Level

Tracing

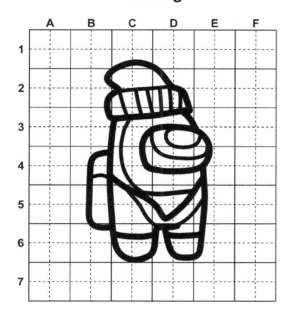

Step 1. Grid Example

Your tract!

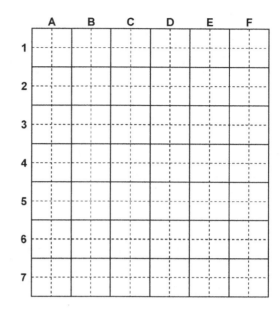

Step 2. Draw Follow Grid Line

Advance Level

Draw it!

Step 1 Image Example

Your own!

Step 2. Draw Follow Image

Beginner Level

Tracing

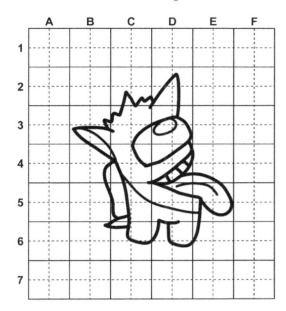

Step 1.Grid Example

Your tract!

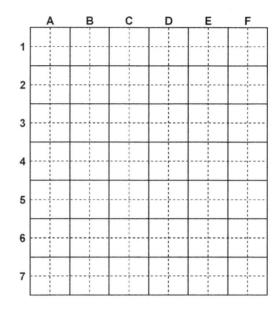

Step 2. Draw Follow Grid Line

Advance Level

Draw it!

Step 1 Image Example

Your own!

Step 2. Draw Follow Image

Beginner Level

Tracing

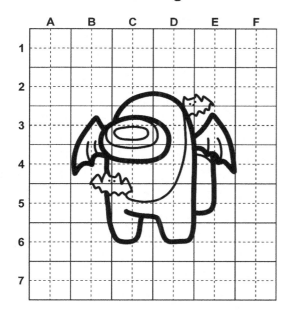

Step 1.Grid Example

Your tract!

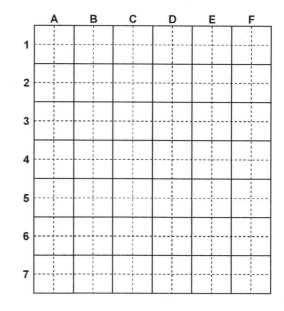

Step 2. Draw Follow Grid Line

Advance Level

Draw it!

Step 1 Image Example

Your own!

Step 2. Draw Follow Image

Beginner Level

Tracing

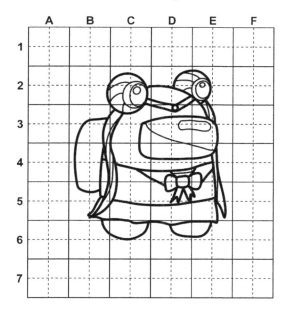

A B C D E F

1 2 3 4 5 6 7

Step 1.Grid Example

Your tract!

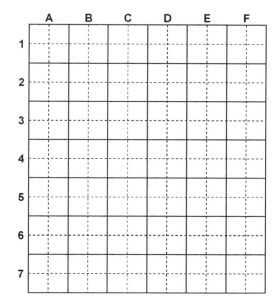

A B C D E F

1 2 3 4 5 6 7

Step 2. Draw Follow Grid Line

Advance Level

Draw it!

Step 1 Image Example

Your own!

Step 2. Draw Follow Image

Beginner Level

Tracing

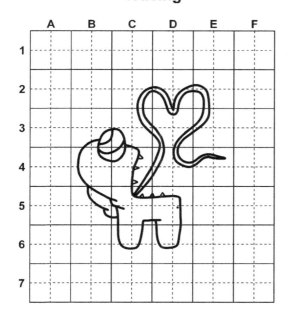

Step 1.Grid Example

Your tract!

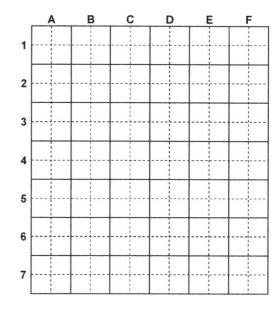

Step 2. Draw Follow Grid Line

Advance Level

Draw it!

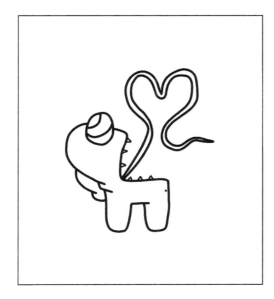

Step 1 Image Example

Your own!

Step 2. Draw Follow Image

AMONG US COLORING PAGE

AMONG US COLORING PAGE

AMONG US COLORING PAGE

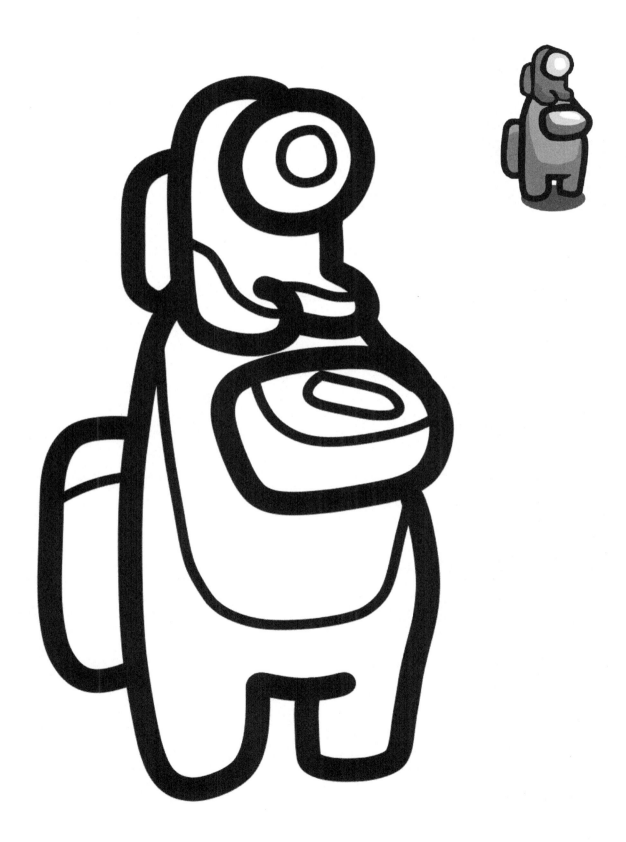

AMONG US COLORING PAGE

AMONG US COLORING PAGE

AMONG US COLORING PAGE

AMONG US COLORING PAGE

AMONG US COLORING PAGE

AMONG US COLORING PAGE

AMONG US COLORING PAGE

AMONG US COLORING PAGE

AMONG US COLORING PAGE

AMONG US COLORING PAGE

AMONG US COLORING PAGE

To parents and kind adults
Thank you

Thank you for reading till the end, it means so much to us that you took your time and make sure that your children learns something from this book. If you have any comments, please do not hesitate to leave it. Your comments will be helpful in creating books in the future. Also, if you enjoyed this book; make sure that you rate us. Lastly I hope you and your family have a good day;.

Contact Us

Email: pjstudio88@gmail.com

Free Bonus

Link Download PDF Files

https://bit.ly/3gVjFNL

Email: pjstudio88@gmail.com

Made in the USA
Coppell, TX
11 January 2021